A HAND FULL OF WATER

for Diana
love
[signature]

April 2018

A HAND FULL OF WATER

TZVETA SOFRONIEVA

TRANSLATED FROM THE GERMAN BY
CHANTAL WRIGHT

WHITE PINE PRESS / BUFFALO, NEW YORK

White Pine Press
P.O. Box 236
Buffalo, New York 14201
www.whitepine.org

State of the Arts

NYSCA

Publication of this book was made possible, in part, by grants
from the Cliff Becker Endowment for the Literary Arts, the
Creative Writing Program at the University of Missouri; and
with public funds from the New York State Council on the Arts,
a State Agency.

The German poems in this volume were first published in *Eine Hand voll Wasser*
(Un Art Ig: Aschersleben, 2008), with the exception of 'Konzert', 'Als Zeus
ihr den Rücken kehrte', 'Der alte Mann, das Meer, die Frau', 'Die Berge, ein
Mann, eine Frau' (*Akzente* 3/2007); 'Rustschuk, Russe, an der Donau' (*Kolik*
45/2009); 'Viadukt' (ICH Verlag Häfner + Häfner: Nürnberg, 2010); 'Hurikan
in Messembria' (*transkrit* 2/2010); 'Der Mann, die Frau, vielleicht ein Meer' and
'wasserkreis' (previously unpublished). The order in which the poems originally
appeared in *Eine Hand voll Wasser* has been altered for this bilingual edition and five
poems have been added.

English translations in this volume have previously appeared in print in
International Poetry Review (Spring 2012), *Exile Quarterly* (34.2, 2010) and *LIT* (15/16,
Winter/Spring 2009), and online at *nth position* (July 2011) and *no man's land* (#5,
2010).

Cover image: *luz con agua 2*. Frame from animation. Copyright © 2005 Eva Davidova

First Edition.

ISBN: 978-1-935210-37-5

Printed and bound in the United States of America.

Library of Congress Number: 2012931169

For Harald

Contents

GESPRÄCH

„Nur trockenes Wasser habe ich nicht getrunken ..."
Joseph Brodsky

Sie:

Dreh dich nicht um im Grab, du begannst,
dem Sein andere Namen zu geben.
Bulgarien werde ich dich nennen,
sagtest du, wie Kleopatra Ägypten war.
Eine Kippe nach der anderen drücktest du
in den Blumentöpfen der Gastgeberin aus,
und auf deiner Stirn funkelte der Schweiß.
Du meintest wieder, ich solle Kavafis lesen,
mir über den Weg nach Ithaka Gedanken machen.
Und gerne wärest du die Frau gewesen, die ich war
und blieb, starke Penelope, die an Ithaka glaubte,
viel mehr an Ithaka und Odysseus als an den Weg.
Dein zielloses Umherirren, deine Visionen,
das Rufen des Lebens zehrten dich aus,
weil sie nur Weg waren. Lass mich dich retten,
ich werde dich Odysseus nennen,
wenigstens im Bild, als mitten im Regen
dein Körper davonging von der Welt,
von mir, ins Nirgendwo, sich aufbäumend,
dass für den Weg Ithaka notwendig ist.
Und dann werde ich die Bücher öffnen,
nebeneinander Homer und dich,
und werde weinen, es wird riechen nach Tabak,
nach Schweiß, nach Mann und nach Tinte.

CONVERSATION

"guzzled everything save dry water ..."
Joseph Brodsky

She:

Don't turn in your grave, you began
to give existence other names.
Said, I shall call you Bulgaria,
just as Cleopatra was called Egypt.
Stubbed out one cigarette after another
in our hostess' flowerpots,
sweat glistening on your forehead.
Told me once again to read Cavafy,
to think about the road to Ithaca.
And you would have liked to be the woman I was
and remained, strong Penelope who believed in Ithaca,
much more in Ithaca and in Odysseus than in the road.
Your aimless wandering, your visions,
life's call exhausted you
because they were merely the road. Let me save you,
I shall call you Odysseus,
at least in the picture where, in the middle of the rain,
your body departed from this world,
from me, into nowhere, rearing up
because Ithaca is necessary for the road.
And then I will open the books,
you and Homer next to each other
and I will cry; it will smell of tobacco,
of sweat, of man and of ink.

Er:

Geh zum Fenster, höre, wie die Wörter fallen.
Wer ist Herbert, wer Auden,
und sollen wir über Rilke reden!
In Venedig bekommt das Wasser seinen poetischen Sinn:
Schau wie die Engel Takt geben —
wie erlaubst du dir ohne Reime zu dichten?
Liebkose die Blätter des Papiers, der Respekt verlangt es.
Hat jemand nach Orpheus auf dem Balkan Verse geschrieben
und was kann nach Achmatova eine Frau überhaupt sagen?

Sie:

Du bist böse, und Sexist bist du,
ein typischer Jude, der nach Westen ausgewandert ist,
du bist der Gott meiner Jugend. Deine Gedichte
leben noch zwischen den Herbstblättern —
wir schrieben sie darauf, überzeugt,
dass uns keiner erwischen könnte,
glaubten an den Zerfall der Materie.
Hier und da Spuren von Tinte:
deine verbotenen ungereimten Gedichte.
Sie blieben mir nicht in Erinnerung,
nur meinen Stoffwechsel haben sie geändert.
Schluss mit der Poesie. Gib mir einen Schluck
aus deiner Tasse Kaffee ohne Zucker.
Ich weiß, du trinkst jetzt auch trockenes Wasser ...

He:

Go to the window, hear how the words fall.
Who is Herbert, who is Auden, and
do we even need to mention Rilke!
In Venice water acquires its poetic meaning:
look how the angels beat out the rhythm—
how dare you write without rhymes?
Caress the sheets of paper, respect demands it.
Has anybody written poetry in the Balkans since Orpheus
and what is there left for a woman to say after Akhmatova?

She:

You're mean, and you're sexist,
a typical Russian Jew who left for the West,
you are the God of my youth. Your poems
live on between the autumn leaves—
we wrote them down there, convinced
no-one could catch us,
we believed in the decay of matter.
Here and there traces of ink:
your forbidden unrhymed poems.
I didn't remember them,
they altered only my metabolism.
Enough poetry. Give me a sip
of your cup of coffee without sugar.
I know you're guzzling dry water now too ...

LANDSCHAFTEN, UFER

Am Meer in Heiligendamm
im Juni, das Wasser, riesig,
silbern, schluckt Haut und
spuckt nackte Menschen aus.

Zwischen den Seen, nördlich davon,
gibt sich die Sonne von alleine hin,
wie nur der Süden sich hingeben kann,
erstaunt dunkeln die Birken.

Am Fluss, östlich,
im Feigenherz reifen Perlen
bernsteinfarbenes Abfinden,
und der Kiesel erstrahlt.

Von der Hoffnung
– dieses schmutzige Wort –
hier, zwischen
Zäunen und Ufern.

LANDSCAPES, SHORE

By the sea in Heiligendamm
in June, the water, gigantic,
silver, eats up skin and
spits out naked bodies.

Between the lakes, to the north,
the sun yields of its own volition,
the way only the south can yield,
the birches darken in amazement.

By the river, to the east,
pearls ripen in fig hearts,
amber-colored resignation,
and the pebbles shine.

With hope
—that dirty word—
here, between
fences and shores.

DER ALTE MANN, DAS MEER, DIE FRAU

I.

Verheiratet ist er seit langem,
liebt, wie es sich gehört,
einmal in der Woche seine Frau
in einer ihrer vielen Verkörperungen,
sonst arbeitet er.
Sie wechselt ihre Haare, Nationalitäten und Jahre,
die Breite der Schenkel und der Betten.
Er bemerkt die Farbe der Bettwäsche nicht.

So leben er und die Frau.

Der einsame, verwöhnte Junge in ihm
beruhigt den alten Mann.
Und der alte Mann ohne das Meer
rudert sein Boot jede Nacht hinaus in die Weite,
dürstet nach dem Fisch.
Und jeden Morgen
schrubbt er das Boot aufs Neue.

Die Frau lässt ihn in Ruhe,
sie sind ja seit langem verheiratet,
wechselt Gesichter, Haare und Nationalitäten,
das Alter, den Preis der Schuhe und die Höhe ihrer Absätze,
die Farbe der Bettwäsche und der Blumen in der Vase.

Das ermüdet ihn manchmal.

Manchmal möchte er die Blumen durch ihren Duft ersetzen
und diesen durch den Jod-Geruch der Algen,
sie aber durch den Geruch von Fisch, Blut und Meer,
durch diesen Gestank, in dem die Frau keinen Platz hat.

THE OLD MAN, THE SEA, THE WOMAN

I.

He's been married a long time
loves, as one should,
his wife once a week
in one of her many forms,
the rest of the time he works.
She changes her hair, nationality and age,
the width of her thighs and of the bed.
He doesn't notice the color of the sheets.

That's how he and the woman live.

The lonely, spoilt boy in him
calms the old man.
And the old man without the sea
rows his boat out every night into the deep,
thirsts for the fish.
And each morning
he scrubs the boat again.

The woman leaves him alone.
they've been married a long time after all,
she changes her face, hair and nationality,
her age, the price of her shoes and the height of their heels,
the color of the sheets and the flowers in the vase.

It tires him sometimes.

Sometimes he'd like to exchange the flowers for their scent
and this scent for the iodine smell of algae,
and these for the smell of fish, blood and sea,
for the stink where the woman has no place.

Sie richtet das Bett mit Wäsche in pompejanischem Rot.
In seinem Bett rauscht das Meer.

2.

Andere Worte bewohnen die anderen Meere.

Und die Boote, die ein Zuhause sein können,
die Zeitungen im Bett.
Und diese Geschichte ist weder die andere Geschichte
noch ist sie
weniger geschehen
oder jemandem weniger
zugehörig.

Hat die Frau eine Geschichte?
Haben die Frau und das Meer eine Geschichte?

3.

Die Frau schwamm lange ins Offene hinaus.
Meerjungfrauen erwarteten sie dort.
Sie schaute sich müde um:
Wo war der alte Mann? Und der Fisch?
Wo war das Boot?
Wo das Meer?

4.

Beschäftigt mit den Angeln und dem Kampf
bemerkte
der alte Mann überhaupt nichts.

She makes their bed with sheets of Pompeian red.
The sea roars in his bed.

2.

Other words inhabit the other seas.

And the boats that could be a home,
the newspapers in bed.
And this story is neither the other story
nor did it
happen any less
nor belong
to anybody less.

Does the woman have a story?
Do the woman and the sea have a story?

3.

The woman swam a long way out into the open.
Mermaids awaited her there.
She looked around tiredly:
Where was the old man? And the fish?
Where was the boat?
The sea?

4.

Busy with the fishing and the struggle
the old man noticed
nothing at all.

5.

Die Frau drehte sich auf den Rücken,
lag entspannt auf den Wellen.
Der Wind wird sie zurückbringen.
Doch vielleicht ziehen die raubgierigen Meeresbewohner
sie dem Fisch des alten Mannes vor
und schließlich siegt er
und kehrt immerhin
mit etwas Fischfleisch nach Hause zurück.

6.

Das Fischskelett und das Boot.
Ihre Leere.
Die Zeitungen. Die Wunden.
Der Junge und seine Erwartung.
Die Frau, war sie auch da oder nicht?

7.

Manchmal träumt er von ihr, und morgens
ist er sicher – er hat vom Meer geträumt.

8.

Er vergisst ihre Verkörperungen,
verzeiht ihr die Liebhaber,
sorgt manchmal für ihr tägliches Brot.
Die Ehe ist eine Art Lösung,
und er ist konsequent.
Der Mensch ändert seine Gewohnheiten nicht,
wenn er alt geworden ist.

5.

The woman turned on her back,
lay relaxed on the waves.
The wind will carry her in.
But maybe the rapacious inhabitants of the sea
will favor her over the old man's fish
and he conquers finally
and in the end returns home
with some fish meat.

6.

The fish skeleton and the boat.
Their emptiness.
The newspapers. The wounds.
The boy and his expectation.
The woman, was she there too or not?

7.

Sometimes he dreams of her, and in the morning
is certain—he dreamed of the sea.

8.

He forgets her many forms,
forgives her the lovers,
sometimes provides her with her daily bread.
Marriage is a kind of solution,
and he sees things through.
Man doesn't change his ways
when he gets old.

Allmählich beginnt der alte Mann zu glauben,
dass der Kampf mit dem Fisch, der Junge
und sogar die Frau
keine Aufgabe sind,
sondern ein Code im Körper.

Gradually the old man starts to believe
that the struggle with the fish, the boy
and even the woman
are not a task
but a code in the body.

DIE BERGE, EIN MANN, EINE FRAU

I.

Wer hat ihn beauftragt, die Berge zu durchwandern?
Niemand. Und genau das macht das Recht des Mannes aus.

Er beneidet die Ureinwohner Australiens
um ihre Heiligen, die man nicht betreten, nie erobern darf.
In Europa strahlen die Berge blau und silbern, weiß und grün.
Sie haben die Geschichten von Geistern aufgegeben, sind
      selten rot.
Nur der Ätna erinnert sich noch mit Glut
an Odysseus und seine Crew.

Der Mann steigt langsam hoch,
atmet tief ein und noch tiefer aus.
Er hat sich gut vorbereitet auf diese Expedition,
ein ganzes Leben lang.

Die Frau ist in Eile, sie ist auf einmal
noch immer und schon wieder jung.
Sie übersieht die Blumen am Wegesrand,
folgt den Lavaspuren, will im Magma baden, ganz oben.
Das Ende des Lebens ist ihr egal.

Eine Frau sorgt sich nie um das Ende, und wäre sie schon alt,
immer nur um den Anfang.

Der Mann geht bedächtig, sucht Steine aus,
redet kaum, wirft Schatten, wenn er auf die Sonne schaut.

Sein Schatten verschmilzt mit dem Schatten des Berges
in den Augen der Frau.
Sie hebt ihre Arme, ihn zu umarmen.
Sie werden Flammen.

The mountains, a man, a woman

I.

Who sent him to walk the mountains?
Nobody. And precisely that characterizes the right of man.

He envies the Aboriginals of Australia their
holy ones, which cannot be climbed, nor conquered.
In Europe the mountains shine blue and silver, white and
     green.
They have surrendered their spirit stories, are seldom red.
Only Etna's embers
remember Odysseus and his crew.

The man ascends slowly,
takes a deep breath in, lets an even deeper breath out.
He has prepared well for this expedition,
his whole life long.

The woman is in a hurry, suddenly she
is still young and young again.
She doesn't see the flowers at the edge of the path,
she follows the lava flows, wants to bathe in magma, up at the top.
She couldn't care less about the end of life.

A woman never worries about the end, and were she old,
only ever about the beginning.

The man treads carefully, chooses his stones,
scarcely speaks, casts shadows when he looks up at the sun.

His shadow merges with the shadow of the mountain
in the woman's eyes.
She lifts her arms to embrace him.
They turn into flames.

2.

Der Mann dürstet immer,
wenn er einen Berg besiegt hat.
Er sehnt sich nach dem Wasser ihrer Brüste
und ihres Mundes.
Sie gibt ihm die Thermoskanne voll Tee,
um wach zu werden.
Sie will ihn haben, wenn sein Durst gestillt ist.

3.

Der Mann liebt die Berge wieder und wieder.
Die Frau liebt den Mann. Die Berge sind ein Teil von ihr.

Liebst du die Berge mehr oder das Meer?
fragt sie.
Berge und Meer, antwortet er.

4.

Oben ist der Schnee versteinert,
versteckt die Lava.
Kristallwüste neben den aus Asche geborenen Felsen,
kaum Luft. Doch Weite
beruhigt die Augen.

Die Frau stürzt sich ins Blaue.
Ein Quantum ist eine Einheit des Lichts
wie eine Schneeflocke eine Einheit des Schnees ist.
Ist ein Tropfen Magma
ein Spiegel dieser Geschichte,
durchfährt es sie während sie fliegend fällt,
wie ein Tropfen Meer
ein Spiegel dieses Berges ist?

2.

The man is always thirsty
when he has conquered a mountain.
He longs for the water of her breasts
and of her mouth.
She gives him the thermos of tea
to revive him.
She will have him once his thirst has been quenched.

3.

The man loves the mountains again and again.
The woman loves the man. The mountains are a part of her.

What do you love more, the mountains or the sea?
she asks.
Mountains and sea, he replies.

4.

At the top the snow has petrified,
conceals the lava.
Crystal desert alongside boulders born of ash,
barely any air. But the vista
calms the eyes.

The woman plunges into the blue.
A quantum is a unit of light
as a snowflake is a unit of snow.
Is a drop of magma
a reflection of this story,
passes through her head as she falls in flight,
as a drop of ocean
is a reflection of this mountain?

Sie erinnert sich an die Zyklopen und an Troja,
wie Achill sich entschied, Geschichte zu werden
und dafür verwundbar zu sein.
An Poseidon und daran,
dass jeder sich mit dem Leben abfinden soll.
An das Meer von Penelope.
Dann ist sie selber schon im Meer und
das Meerwasser dürstet nach ihren Wünschen.

5.

An Orpheus und seine Berge, an seine Lieder
erinnert sich ihr Körper,
an die Kindheit.

Vom Meer aus wirken die Berge
wie schlafende Katzen, zusammengerollt
in ihre eigenen Schultern und Pfoten,
jeden Moment bereit aufzustehen.

Sie schmiegt ihren Hals an die Glätte des Wassers.
Es wird kühl im Meer.

6.

Der Mann
oben auf dem Berg
beobachtet.

Die Frau hat überlebt,
das freut ihn.

Der Sturz war richtig,
sie taucht gern hinein.

She thinks of the Cyclopes and Troy,
how Achilles decided to become history
and rendered himself vulnerable for it.
Of Poseidon and
the fact that everybody should accept their lot.
Of Penelope's sea.
Then she herself is in the sea and
the sea water thirsts for her wishes.

5.

Orpheus and his mountains, his songs
are what her body remembers,
childhood.

From the sea the mountains look like
sleeping cats, curled up
into their shoulders and paws,
ready to rise at any moment.

She nuzzles her neck against the smoothness of the water.
The sea is growing cold.

6.

The man
on the mountain
watches.

The woman has survived,
that's good.

She was right to fall,
she likes to dive.

Der Mann wünscht, der Schnee wäre Lava.

Er wird jetzt hinab laufen,
vielleicht kommt er an.

7.

Die Frau kommt ans Ufer, friert im Schatten des Berges.
Warum war er nicht mit ihr gesprungen?

8.

Die Frau verzeiht seine Zeitnot,
ist ja schon lange an ihn gewöhnt.
Der Mann bereitet sein Sterben vor
und sein Leben nach dem Tod.
Sie will, dass er heute bleibt.

Die Frau speichert die Gerüche seiner Umarmung.
Umwickelt von den Seilen seiner Sehne
und seinem Sehnen
beginnt sie die Geschichte ohne ihn zu leben.

Die Schatten der Berge auf der Oberfläche der Wellen
und in ihren Augen
bleiben.

The man wishes the snow were lava.

He's going to descend now,
perhaps he'll make it.

7.

The woman reaches the shore, freezes in the shadow of the
        mountain.
Why didn't he jump with her?

8.

The woman forgives his hurry,
she has grown used to him.
The man is preparing his death
and his life after death.
She'd like him to stay today.

The woman memorizes the smells of his embrace.
Wrapped in the cord of his ligaments
and his longing
she begins to live her story without him.

The shadows of the mountains on the surface of the waves
and in her eyes
remain.

GEWOHNHEITEN

Ich kann mich nicht lieben
Deswegen liebe ich mir ähnelnde Menschen

Hörte ich von einem Mädchen mit orangenen Haaren
an einem verblassenden Abend

Sie hieß Klara und war
ein wie Kristall klares Wesen —
ich glaube, sie heißt noch immer so,
malt mit viel Farbe und Wasser,
liebt Professoren

An meinem Fenster klopfen sich ausbreitende Bäume
Ich muss nachdenken, ob ich mich selbst liebe

verzeihe ich mir das Zittrige, die Dämmerungen,
die vertanen Versuche, meinen Herzschlag zu fangen

Ich lasse mich auf den Charme chaotischer Freundschaften
        ein,
werde von uralten Gesten angezogen,

im Rythmus eines neuen Spiels
radiere ich Worte und schreibe Gedichte
diiiiicht iiiiiichtdi

HABITS

I can't love myself
that's why I love people like me

was something I heard from a girl with orange hair
on an evanescent evening

Her name was Clara, she was
a clear being, like crystal—
I think that's still her name,
she paints with lots of color and water,
adores professors

Outstretched trees knock at my window
I will have to consider whether I love myself

whether I can forgive myself the nervousness, the twilight
     realizations,
the abortive attempts to catch my heartbeat

I am seduced by the charm of chaotic friendships
and attracted by ancient gestures

In the rhythm of a new game
I erase words and write lines
I wr I te l I nes I wr I

KONZERT

Wasser. Atem holen. Kann nicht geholt werden.
Hauch, Wellen, Violine.
Klänge. Können nicht getrunken, nicht geatmet werden.
Kleben im Haar. Tiefe Männerstimme.
Provokation, die Erinnerung an die Bretagne,
wo ich nie war.
Tropfen auf den Schultern zweier Frauen, Wasser,
ihre Haut, Babyhaut, Greisinnenhaut,
weibliche Haut. Du solltest in mir sein.
Die Sehnsucht nach der Küste der Bretagne,
wo sie diese Musik schrieb, der Sand und du in mir,
deine Lieder in meinem Haar, fließt in die Augen über,
Klänge wie die der Mutter, der Großmutter, Sehnsucht –
eine banale Verflechtung aus Geige und Gewobenem,
ein Webstuhl aus Saiten, schwebt über dem Wasser
der Bretagne,
dort, auf der Grenze zwischen Wasser und Nebel,
ist jeder Zufall ausgeschlossen. Wie damals,
als ich dort war – ein Kind mit einer Violine,
ich konnte spielen und malen.
Deine Augen waren voller Klänge.
Sie spielt Violine, und ich erinnere mich
An die Bretagne, wo ich nie war.

Ihr Kleid ist weiß und silbern.
Die Menschen klatschen.

CONCERT

Water. Catch your breath. Cannot be caught.
Breeze, waves, violin.
Sounds. Cannot be drunk or breathed.
Sticky hair. Deep male voice.
Provocation, the memory of Brittany,
where I've never been.
Drops on the shoulders of two women, water,
their skin, baby skin, old lady skin,
female skin. You should be inside me.
Yearning for the coast of Brittany
where she wrote this music, the sand and you inside me,
your songs in my hair, spills over into the eyes,
sounds like the ones mother, grandmother made, yearning—
a banal mesh of violin and weave,
a loom of strings, floats over the water
in Brittany,
there, on the border between water and mist,
there can be no coincidence. When
I was there—a child with a violin,
I could play and paint.
Your eyes were full of sounds.
She is playing the violin, and I remember
Brittany, where I've never been.

Her dress is white and silver.
The people clap.

HURIKAN IN MESSEMBRIA

Nessebar explodiert, die Kirchen zerfallen,
haben längst vergessen, das Meer zu lieben.
Der Seetang tanzt auf Flügeln der Mühle,
bewegt sie besser als der Wind.
Touristen verstecken sich im nahen Kurort,
der Strand ist magnetisiert von der Begegnung,
Haie nagen zum nächtlichen Mahl am Sand
und verkünden: Der Vollmond ist verschoben worden.
Der Mond versteckt sich in dem Schleier des Sturmes
inmitten von dreckigen Wolken aus Dampf und Krebsen,
wir verblassen im Wirbel der Gefühle,
bei dem sich sogar die alten Steine verschieben.
Nessebar wartete nicht ab, um langsam verschlungen zu werden,
stürzte sich selbst ins Meer.
Lange werden wir Spuren im Sand suchen,
die einen Sinn beweisen.

HURRICANE IN MESEMBRIA

Nesebar is exploding, the churches are crumbling,
have long since forgotten to love the sea.
Seaweed waltzes on the windmill's paddles,
propels them faster than the wind.
The tourists hide in a nearby resort,
the beach is magnetized by its encounter,
sharks gnaw at the sand for their evening meal
and proclaim: the full moon has been postponed.
The moon hides in the veil of the storm
within dirty clouds of haze and crabs,
we pale in the swell of feelings,
even the old stones shift position.
Nesebar didn't wait to be swallowed by degrees,
threw itself into the sea.
We'll go on seeking clues in the sand
that point to meaning.

FÜR EUROPA WERBEN

Wir haben uns nirgendwo getroffen,
zusammen frühstücken wollten wir immer,
den frühen Kaffee riechen, uns kennen lernen.
„Guten Morgen!" Europa brodelt.
Ein wenig zugefügter Schaum. Verführte Ränder.
Es dreht sich ein cremiger Tornado,
nur in der Mitte bleibt ein schwarzer Streifen
(Espresso, express, gepresst?)
Wir werden schneller als vermutet alt.
Genuss. Eine Versuchung der Vereinigung,
gewollte Träume im Voraus.
Orgasmen kann man sich vorstellen,
auch unerlebte leben –
solche, in denen Völker
Verfassungen im kollektiven Rausch entscheiden.
Und du beschwörst mich, neue Orte zu beleben.
(Gestern erst wollte ich das Leben aufgeben.)
Auf meinen Lippen tanzen Zellen,
unartige, vermehren sich exponentiell.
Das Leben wählen, sagst du, schnell
sich zur Langsamkeit bekennen.
Und für die Erweiterung der Zukunft werben.

COURTING EUROPE

We met nowhere
but we always wanted to have breakfast,
smell the early morning coffee, get acquainted.
"Good morning!" Europe splutters.
A little extra foam. Seduction at the rim.
A creamy tornado builds in a cup,
a lone black stripe at the center
(espresso, express, French press?)
We age faster than we think.
Pleasure. Attemptation of union,
an advance on wished-for dreams.
We can conceive of orgasms,
even experience some that never took place—
those where peoples
pass constitutions in a collective frenzy.
And you charm me into inhabiting new places.
(Only yesterday I was ready to give up on life.)
Mischievous cells dance on my lips,
multiply exponentially.
Choose life, you say, quickly
commit to slowness.
And court the expansion of the future.

ES KOMMT EIN SCHIFF GELADEN

Das ist die Geschichte der Leidenschaft
und die Leidenschaft der Geschichte.

Sie fehlt mir, sie fehlt mir nicht, sie fehlt mir.
Die südliche Musik wendet meine Haut,
und ich bin da in einem anderen Licht:
die Schenkel – Muskelstränge und Fett,
die Hüften – Knochen, die die Gebärmutter halten,
die Brüste – sich zusammenziehende Lungen,
die Lippen – Endungen von schluckenden Klappen,
die Haare – verlängerte Gehirnhäute.
Wir haben mindestens zwei Gesichter schon bei der Empfängnis.

Das Orakel von Delphi hat Europas Renaissance verflucht.
Diese Stadt kann nicht gleichzeitig Solun und Thessaloniki sein,
wir gehören nicht zwei Welten.
Unsere Segel versanken ins Meer,
das weder das Schwarze noch das Weiße war.
Wir erreichten Land bei Smyrna, oder war es Izmir?
Pergamon und Ephesos strahlen Wellen und Schritte aus.

Wer zeugt die Geschichte?
Und wer hat das Monopol, davon zu erzählen?

A SHIP IT COMES A-LADEN

This is the history of passion
and the passion of history.

She loves me, she loves me not, she loves me.
The southern music turns my skin,
and I stand there in a different light:
my thighs—skeins of muscle with fat,
my hips—bones that enclose my womb,
my breasts—contracting lungs,
my lips—the tips of hungry valves,
my hair—the extension of my cerebral membranes.
We have at least two faces when we are conceived.

The oracle at Delphi cursed Europe's renaissance.
This city cannot be both Solun and Thessaloniki,
we don't belong to two worlds.
Our sails sank into a sea
which was neither the Black nor the White.
We reached land at Smyrna, or was it Izmir?
Pergamon and Ephesus radiate waves and steps.

Who creates history?
And who has the monopoly on its telling?

EINE HAND VOLL WASSER

Wir wandern in der Sprache, wir wandern,
и не земя, вода на длан ни е нужна,
denn wir haben gelernt, durstig zu sein.
Vom Wasser haben wir's gelernt, vom Wasser.
Das hat nicht Ruh bei Tag und Nacht,
ist stets auf Wanderschaft bedacht, das Wasser.

Die Sprache ist wie Wasser.
Beim Halten verliert man sie,
im Fließen hat sie Bestand,
schenkt eher Leben als Ertrinken,
wäscht keine Flecken aus,
ist der erste Grund, dass alles keimen kann.

Тръгнала Румяна за вода студена, леле,
тръгнала Румяна за вода студена.
Живата вода търсила, леле, живата.
Wasser wollte die junge Frau holen, Wasser,
kalt sollte es sein, lebendig, das Wasser.
Entgegen kommt ihr ein junger Mann, will
von ihren Krügen trinken, ihr Liebe schwören.
Man braucht keine Krüge, sagt sie ihm,
um Wasser zu trinken.
Das Wasser ist wie die Sprache.

Nimm keine Kelle, keinen Becher.
Nimm keine Handvoll.
Trinke direkt von der Quelle.
И я остави на мира, водата,
и го остави на мира, езика,
und lass mich endlich,
Worte und Grammatik schreiben,
wie ich empfinde.

A HAND FULL OF WATER

We wander through language, we wander,
и не земя, вода на длан ни е нужна,
for we have learned to thirst.
We learned it from the water, the water
That knows no rest by day or night
Forever picturing its flight, the water.

Language is like water.
In stasis it slips away,
in flow it finds its form,
feeds more than it drowns,
will not wash away stains,
is the reason shoots emerge.

Тръгнала Румяна за вода студена, леле,
тръгнала Румяна за вода студена.
Живата вода търсила, леле, живата.
Water, the young woman wanted water,
cold and lively, the water.
A young man came her way, wanted
to drink from her vessels, profess his love.
You do not need a vessel, she said,
to drink water.
Water is like language.

Do not take a ladle, do not take a cup,
do not take a handful.
Drink from the source.
И я остави на мира, водата,
и го остави на мира, езика,
and please let me
use words and grammar
as I see fit.

Und
lasst es in Frieden weiterziehen,
das Wasser,
und lasst sie in Frieden weiterziehen und wandern,
die Sprache,
und lasst mich in Frieden
weiter
ziehen,

lasst mich in Frieden weiterziehen,
in Frieden weiterziehen und wandern.

And
let it take its leave,
the water,
and let language take its leave,
and wander,
and let me
take my
leave,

let me take my leave,
take my leave and wander.

UN-LOST IN TRANSLATION

Im Fenster vorn rechts in meinem Abteil
spiegelt sich das linke hintere Bild.
Ich sehe im Kommenden das Entrinnende
völlig überlagert, und es ist als ob das Licht
dieses Spiel mag, unabhängig davon, wo
die Sonne steht und wohin der Zug reist.

Un-lost in Translation

The window at the front and right of my compartment
reflects the scene on the left at my rear.
I can see what is passing superimposed on
what is coming, and it is as though the light
likes this game, irrespective of where the sun is
or where the train is heading.

NOCH EINES DER VERBOTENEN WORTE

wenn du nicht ein engel wärest hätte ich dich geliebt
deinen körper verschluckt millimetergenau die erde erkundet
wenn du einen körper hättest
zu nahe wärest du mir dann du wärest kein engel
sauerstoff brennt
man verbrennt sich an stickstoff der nicht brennt
engel brennen
man verbrennt sich an menschen die nicht brennen
pathos ist tatsächlich etwas altmodisches
pathos und engel passen gut zusammen
wenn du kein engel wärest hätte ich dich geliebt
agressiv wie frauen männer lieben die keine engel sind
das tun die frauen und sie tun es wieder und wieder
flüssiger stickstoff ist immer eine zumutung
er ist nämlich kein stoff hat falten tut weh
wird nebel wird dunst wird finster wird ersticken
sehnsucht
verschwinde nicht

ANOTHER ONE OF THOSE FORBIDDEN WORDS

if you were not an angel i would have loved you
devoured your body by the millimeter explored the earth
if you had a body
you would be too close to me you wouldn't be an angel then
oxygen burns
you burn yourself on nitrogen that doesn't burn
angels burn
you burn yourself on people who don't burn
pathos is old-fashioned
pathos and angels go well together
if you weren't an angel i would have loved you
aggressively the way women love men who aren't angels
that's what women do and they do it over and over again
liquid nitrogen is always presumptive
has nothing of the elemental, evaporates and causes pain
turns to mist, to haze, to darkness, can drown
longing
stay

SONNE

Zeichnest Augen und Augenbrauen,
stichst nichts aus,
sanft, leuchtend, brennst,
kannst nicht ausbrennen.
Schwingst wie ein Vogel,
fliegst vom Gesicht
des Fahrenden ab.
Nach Osten fährt er.
Zartes Feuer,
ich liebkose dich,
noch lebe ich.
Keine Spur Asche oder Durst.
Eine Kinderzeichnung bist du
Sonne

SUN

Who draws eyes and eyebrows
who makes no incisions,
gentle, luminous, who burns,
who can't burn out.
Who swings like a bird,
who flies away from the face
of the traveler.
He's going east.
Tender fire,
I caress you,
I am still alive.
No trace of ash or thirst.
You are a child's drawing
sun

WASSERKREIS

es kommen wieder tropfen auf uns zu
befeuchten sand verschwinden
die töchter spielen doktor
spielen körper
du bringst mir norden regen
bogen schnee und wieder tropfen
aufatmen
atmen tropfen aus
schweiß verzweifeln
dunkle höhle unter betten
so einfach existiert die welt
eine vagina im wasserspiegel

WATER CYCLE

more drops are heading our way
wet the sand disappear
the daughters play doctor
play bodies
you bring me north rain
bow snow more drops
to breathe again
breathe out drops
of sweat despair
dark cave under beds
the world exists so simply
a vagina in a mirror of water

Der Mann, die Frau, vielleicht ein Meer

1.

Die Oberfläche soll ein Spiegel sein,
dann trifft man Wale und Delfine.
Bei Wind gehen die Wellen ihren Spielen nach,
die Meeressiedler sind leicht zu übersehen.
Der Mann wünscht sich bauchige Segel,
die Frau begehrt die Windstille.

2.

Am Hafen bereitet der Mann einen Schwertfisch,
die Frau breitet Schals und Netze gegen Insekten aus.
Mücken und Falter überschwemmen das Boot.
Der Mann fürchtet kein Insekt,
nur die neue Funktion der Seile.
Ein Stich trifft sein Augenlid zum Beweis der Furcht.

3.

Napoleon, Piratenschlacht, die drei Musketiere,
der Sonnenstaat, die Orionnacht,
ein Korsika T-Shirt auf einem Elba-Strand,
Monte Christo im Privatbesitz,
die Frau ist trotzdem nicht bereit,
ihre Kindheitsträume aufzugeben.
Sie brechen wieder auf.

THE MAN, THE WOMAN, PERHAPS A SEA

1.

The surface needs to be a mirror,
you see whales and dolphins then.
When it's windy the waves pursue their games,
it's easy to miss the sea dwellers.
The man wishes for full-bellied sails,
the woman longs for calm.

2.

The man prepares a swordfish in the harbour,
the woman unfurls shawls and nets against the insects.
Gnats and moths flood the boat.
The man isn't afraid of insects,
just the repurposing of the rope.
A sting to the eyelid is proof of his fear.

3.

Napoleon, a pirate battle, the three musketeers,
City of the Sun, Orion night,
a Corsica T-shirt on an Elba beach,
Monte Cristo in private hands,
all the same the woman is not prepared,
to forego her childhood dreams.
They set off again.

4.

Frau und Mann wechseln sich als Navigatoren ab.
Das Kind wird später vom lauten Ankerwerfen geweckt,
von dieser Kette, die hin und her schlägt
und das Meeresrauschen bestätigt.

Aber erst bei jener Bucht,
von der man immer wieder aufbrechen kann,
ankommen.

5.

Hafen oder Bucht,
das ist oft im Offenen
die wichtigste Entscheidung.

4.

Woman and man take turns at navigation.
Later the child is woken by the noise of throwing anchor,
by the chain, clanking back and forth,
confirming the noise of the sea.

But only on arrival in the bay
from where one can always set sail
again.

5.

Often the most important decision
out in the open
is harbour or bay.

Das Schliessen der Fakultät für Südslawistik

Lange war ich außerhalb des Lebens,
war in einem anderen Leben:
in meinem eigenen.
Immer wieder kehrte ich nach Sofia zurück
als eine neue Auswanderungswelle rollte
und verstand nicht, was passierte.
Sogar nach Plowdiv reiste ich und letztlich
kam ich bis nach Tarnovo und Russe,
was nicht viel geholfen hat.
Aber die Flüsse und die Berge des Balkans
lieben sich leidenschaftlich weiter —
das kann man über den Westen Europas
nicht mehr behaupten, denn dort gibt es
viel zu viele Brücken über Täler und Tiefen.

Das Buch von Foucault ist '89
auf dem Postweg verloren gegangen,
und die amerikanische Kollegin,
die mir dieses Buch schenkte,
starb sehr jung einige Jahre danach,
so kamen weder seine noch ihre Sätze
am Balkan an. Aber heute macht das nichts aus.

Der Feta, genauer gesagt *бялото саламурено сирене*,
der sich vom Feta unterscheidet,
weil er auch im ungesalzenen Wasser ruhen soll,
und sich auch vom Schafskäse unterscheidet,
weil er auch aus Kuh- oder Ziegenmilch
gemacht werden kann,

dieser Feta also ist ein herrliches Ding
in Salaten
und noch herrlicher ist

THE CLOSURE OF THE FACULTY FOR SOUTH-EAST EUROPEAN STUDIES

For a long time I was outside life,
in another life:
my own.
I always returned to Sofia
as a new wave of emigration was unfurling
and failed to understand what was going on.
I even travelled to Plovdiv and then
to Tarnovo and Rousse;
it didn't help much.
But the rivers and the mountains of the Balkans
still love each other passionately—
the same cannot be maintained
of Western Europe, where there are
far too many bridges over valleys and deeps.

The Foucault book went missing
in the post, in '89,
and the American colleague
who sent me the book
died very young several years later,
so neither his sentences nor hers ever
made it to the Balkans. But that doesn't matter now.

Feta, or more precisely *бялото саламурено сирене*,
which is not the same as feta
because it sits in unsalted water,
and is not the same as sheep's cheese
because you can make it
from cow's or goat's milk too,

well, this feta is a wonderful thing
in salads
and what is even more wonderful is

der dicke saure Jogurt, weiß, mit Messern zu schneiden,
der auf der Zunge zergeht.

(Ohne dass darauf zwingend folgend würde,
dass der fließende Brie oder der Koriander
in Sojasoße die Zunge unbefriedigt lassen.
Dimitar K. wird damit nicht einverstanden,
Dimitar S. dagegen wird einverstanden sein.)

Wenn du das, was dein Land durchmacht,
davor erlebt hast, ist viel Warten angesagt.
Es scheint mir, dass ich von geschlossenen Jeeps
mit dem Aussehen einer Luxus-Karosse, keine
Ahnung habe, weiß nur, dass mit so einem Jeep
von jeher in Wüsten und Steppen gereist wird.
Und für mich bedeuten die Städte immer noch
Menschen, Menschen, Menschen.

Langsam werden wir alle pensionslose Rentner
(auf das Wort arbeitslos verzichten alle
Workaholiker), und zum Abschied trinken wir
ein Glas Wein aus den Rhodopen.
Jede Weisheit sammelt Traurigkeit ist nur
ein Spruch aus der Bibel — die Erfahrung macht heiter,
sagt Dionysos und schließt sich uns an.

the thick, sour yoghurt, white, sliced with a knife,
that melts on the tongue.

(Without necessarily implying
that runny Brie or coriander
in soy sauce leave the tongue unsatisfied.
Dimitar K. will disagree,
Dimitar S., on the other hand, will agree.)

When you have already experienced
what your country is going through,
waiting is the order of the day.
I seem not to understand covered jeeps
that look like luxury carriages,
I only know that this kind of jeep
was always used to travel deserts and the steppes.
And for me cities still mean
people, people, people.

Gradually we are all turning into pensionless pensioners
(all workaholics avoid the word
unemployed), and in farewell we drink
a glass of wine from the Rhodopes.
With wisdom comes sorrow is just
a quotation from the Bible—experience makes merry,
says Dionysus, and joins our crew.

ALS ZEUS IHR DEN RÜCKEN KEHRTE

Die Sprache, die mein Zuhause war,
ist heute eine Feder in Europas Flügeln:
Wird die Schöne fliegen oder sich nur
narzisstisch in der Quelle spiegeln?

When Zeus turned his back on her

The language that used to be my home
is now a feather in Europa's wings:
Will she fly or admire her own beauty,
narcissistically, in the spring?

EIN UNBEKANNTES WORT

Носталгия ist ein Fremdwort:
Homesickness, Heimweh, Nostalgie.
Auf Bulgarisch existiert das Wort nicht
und meine Tochter sagte gestern:
Мамо, имам Heimweh за теб.
Der Ort des Bewohnens kann Berlin sein,
Beverly Hills, Bitterfeld, Konska, Paris.
Hauptsache es riecht nach Mama,
nach ihren immer schneller alternden Händen,
die mit Uhus reden können
und stark umarmen.

Wer kommt in meine Arme?
Den hab ich lieb!

Я кажи ми, облаче ле бяло,
отгде идеш, що си ми видяло,
не видя лиии ...
Wer kommt, erwartet und geliebt,
in meine Flügel, die eines Kolibris?

Kommt ein Vogel geflogen ...
Гугутка гука в усои, леле,
гукни ми гукни, гугутке,
гукни ми гукни пай пукни, леле,
и аз така съм гукала, хееей,
home, home, sweet home.
Ein Täubchen singt in der Hecke,
ich habe auch so gesungen
als ich bei Mama aufwuchs.
Oh, when my mom combed me
my hair grew long.
Ach, als Mutter mich wusch,

AN UNKNOWN WORD

Носталгия is a strange word:
homesickness, Heimweh, Nostalgie.
In Bulgarian the word does not exist
and yesterday my daughter said:
Мамо, имам Heimweh за теб.
You can live in Berlin,
Beverly Hills, Bitterfeld, Konska, Paris,
as long as it smells of Mom
and her rapidly aging hands
that can commune with owls
and hold you tight.

I feel her arms a huggin' me
As when she held me then.

Я кажи ми, облаче ле бяло,
отгде идеш, що си ми видяло,
не видя лиии ...
And I hear her voice a hummin'
Too ra loo ra loo ral, too ra loo ra li.

Kommt ein Vogel geflogen ...
Гугутка гука в усои, леле,
гукни ми гукни, гугутке,
гукни ми гукни пай пукни, леле,
и аз така съм гукала, хееей,
home, home, sweet home.
A little dove is singing
in tones so sweet and low,
as I did with momma, so many years ago.
Ach, als Mutter mich wusch,
strahlte mein Gesicht.
Oh, when my mom combed me

strahlte mein Gesicht.
Du, Vögelein, singe wie damals,
sing, sing, blow up and die.
Sick, sick, weh, weh, heim, heim.

Ein Wort des Vermissens.

Abwesenheit und Sehnsucht — gefährlich.
Schmerz für Daheim, Zuhause-Krankheit.
Sitzt man da unbeweglich?
Aber es gibt auch Aufbruch, Asyl, Fremdwohnen,
Ein- und Auswandern, *изгнание, гурбет,*
хъшове, странстване, Wege.
Der Mensch geht und kommt, um wieder zu gehen.
Und auf dem Weg
erreicht das Zurückkehren
auf der anderen Seite das Abbrechen.
Das ist es.
Ein sich drehender Kreis.
Ich habe nie daran gedacht,
Worte der Zugehörigkeit oder Anerkennung
zu gebrauchen.

my hair grew long.
Little bird, Vögelein, sing as you did then,
sing, sing, blow up and die.
Sick, sick, weh, weh, heim, heim.

A word about missing things.

Absence and longing—dangerous.
A homeache, Zuhause-Krankheit.
Are we so inflexible?
But there is also leaving home, seeking asylum, living abroad,
Ein- und Auswandern, изгнание, гурбет,
хъшове, странстване, Wege.
People come and go so they can leave again.
And en route
arrival catches up with departure
on the other side of the road.
It is what it is.
A revolving circle.
It has never occurred to me
to use
words of acceptance or belonging.

Die Rückkehr des weissen Stiers

Im Meer bei Ithaka, in der Kühle der Wellen,
wo das durchsichtige Wasser jedes Geheimnis offenbart,
wie Blätterteig gefaltete, krustige Felsen,
eine Bibliothek von Epen,
ich esse sie mit den Augen.

Da ist er, weiß, wutschnaubend,
der Gehörnte ist wieder vorwärtsstrebend.
Die Anmutige verlässt den Mythos,
um ihm zu entkommen.
Er stürmt voran, überspringt die Berge,
will sie wie einst nehmen
mit der Zuversicht des Gottes.
Damals ihm hingegeben
will sie heute einen anderen.
Grün sind Apollos Augen.
Der Stier stürmt weiter voran
und als er das Meer erreicht,
trinkt er, reißt den Boden auf.

Die Segel unseres Bootes flattern,
in dem Kanal zwischen Meganisi und Lefkas
gibt es wenig Wind, der Tag ist heiß und trocken.
Wir segeln zu jener Insel, ersehnt
so viele Jahre von Odysseus,
so viele Jahre von anderen nach ihm
und um so viele mehr von mir.
Der Kapitän will uns an andere Ufer bringen,
die Götter sind nicht mit uns, sagt er,
die Winde sind ungünstig, hör auf mit deinem Ithaka.
Und ich starre in den Meeresdunst,
unaufhaltsam sehne ich mich
nach jenen Ufern.

THE RETURN OF THE WHITE BULL

In the sea by Ithaca, in the cool of the waves
where the clear water reveals every secret,
crusty rocks folded over like puff pastry,
a library of epics,
I eat them with my eyes.

There he is, white, snorting anger,
the horned beast is on the move again.
The gracious woman exits the myth
to escape him.
He charges onwards, leaps over the mountains,
wants to take her as he did once before
with all the confidence of a god.
She gave herself to him then,
today she wants somebody else.
Apollo's eyes are green.
The bull continues his charge
and when he reaches the sea
he drinks, tears the ground apart.

The sails on our boat flutter,
in the canal between Meganisi and Lefkas
there is little wind, the day is hot and dry.
We sail to the island yearned after
for so many years by Odysseus
for so many years by others after him
and for even more by me.
The captain wants to bring us to other shores,
the gods are not with us, he says,
the winds are unfavorable, will you please stop talking about
    Ithaca.
I stare into the haze of the sea,
I long incessantly
for those shores.

Das Ionische Meer erkennt mich,
und alle Reisen von Odysseus bin ich schon gereist,
und habe den Zorn Poseidons nicht geweckt,
womit auch? –
und keiner wartet auf mich in Ithaka,
es wird Zeit für mich, dort anzukommen.
Der Kapitän trinkt „Mythos" Bier,
öffnet die Karten,
seine Falten zeichnen sich aus dem Gebräunten,
ich verspreche ein Gedicht, er lenkt ein.
Und als die Entscheidung fällt, dreht der Wind,
hetzt das Boot immer wilder,
und wir, die Füße fest am Boot,
halten kaum das Steuer ...

Wir kommen an, und drei Tage je drei Mal versuchen wir dort
Anker bei den Olivenstämmen zu werfen.
Und in drei Buchten lächelt uns Ithaka freundlich zu
und stößt uns ab,
der Anker gleitet ab im Seetang und greift nicht.

Lass uns mindestens schwimmen springen
Der Kapitän wird rufen:
„Du zuerst,
küss das heilige Wasser!"
Und sein Scherz wird zu weiteren drei zornigen Tagen führen,
in den drei Buchten,
und noch drei mal drei.

The Ionian Sea recognizes me,
and I have journeyed all of Odysseus' routes
and did not arouse Poseidon's anger,
how would I?—
and nobody is waiting for me in Ithaca,
it is time for me to reach its shore.
The captain is drinking Mythos beer,
opens up the charts,
the lines on his face draw themselves into his tan,
I promise a poem, he comes around.
And as the decision is made, the wind changes,
rocks the boat even more wildly,
and we, our feet anchored to the deck,
can scarcely hold the rudder ...

We arrive, and three times on each of three days we try
to drop anchor next to the olive logs.
And in three bays Ithaca gives us a friendly smile
and pushes us away,
the anchor slides in seaweed and refuses to grip.

Let's go for a swim at least.
The captain shouts:
"You first,
kiss the holy water!"
And his joke will lead to three more angry days
in the three bays,
and a further three times three.

Taufe

Wir mieten von der Welt ein Sofa, eine Tür,
ein Kissen, einen Obstbaum, Flügel und ein Boot,
nennen es *Zuhause*, fügen mehrere Namen ein.
Morgen ist die Stadt neu, die Gesichter,
die Fenster, die Wellen, das Licht und die Kiesel,
in denen das Wasser Widerstand findet.
Wir mieten uns einen Steg, einen Fluss, Metropolenglimmer,
eine Zeremonie, den Priester und die singenden Nonnen,
Münzen, heilige Weide, Grenzen des Ichs, Zunge, Teller
und Gewürze für die Zunge, exotische Orte und uralte Zeiten.
Verzehren es langsam. Und stehen vor einer neuen Taufe.
Und viele Arten Wasser warten auf uns. Und jedes Mal
erschreckt uns die Berührung mit dem Taufbecken.

BAPTISM

We rent a sofa, a door, a pillow, a fruit tree,
wings and a boat from the world,
call them *home*, dispose of several names.
Tomorrow the city is new, the faces,
the windows, the waves, the light and the pebbles
where water finds resistance.
We rent a landing stage, a river, metropolitan glimmer,
a ceremony, the priest and singing nuns,
coins, sacred pasture, borders of the self, tongue, plate
and spices for the tongue, exotic places and ancient times.
Consume them slowly. And are faced with a new baptism.
And many kinds of water await us. And each time
we are shocked when we enter the baptismal pool.

Einbürgerung am Valentinstag

die bräuche sind andere, einfach andere
bräuche

bräuchte, erst brauchte ich
hätte ich, habe ich gebraucht
dich lange genug zu lieben

mein wort
deine stadt

aus deinem ort ein wort in mir zu machen

das bett drei jahre
und beweise über die herkunft
        des ehegatten oder der ehegattin
kein pass, benötigt werden: die nummer
der einheit, in der sein bzw. ihr vater
        in der deutschen armee gedient hat
(mit der absicht, meinen vater zu töten)
und der einheit, in der sein bzw. ihr großvater
        in der deutschen armee gedient hat
(gegen meinen großvater)
nichts anderes beweist die europäische zugehörigkeit
des deutschen
bettes

die idee alles allein zu meistern: 10 jahre lang
gut verdienen
miete ohne rückstände bezahlen
bedeutet deutsch zu sein
das ist alles
wortzeugen sind nicht zu gebrauchen

Attaining citizenship on Valentine's Day

things are different, simply
different

things i would need, first i would need
first i would have to, i needed
to love you long enough

my word
your city

to turn your world into a word in me

a bed for three years
and proof of the nationality
            of one's spouse
no passport; the requirements are: the number
of the unit in which his/her father
            served in the german army
(with intent to kill my father)
and the unit in which his/her grandfather
            served in the german army
(against my grandfather)
nothing else will prove the european citizenship of the german
bed

the idea
mastering everything by oneself: 10 years of
earning well
paying rent with no arrears
means you are german
that's it
wordwitnesses have no role to play

und keinesfalls reicht es, ein deutsches kind geboren zu haben
frau sein ist sowieso nicht deutsch
eine mutter zu haben beweist keine zugehörigkeit
mütter gebären nur
sie zeugen nichts
sie können keine zeugen sein

aus deinem wort einen ort in mir zu machen

wie lange ist lange genug für die liebe?

fangen wir mit 13 an
weil es seit jeher abergläubisch klingt

ohne bett und ohne geld
nur das land meines zufälligen umherirrens
meiner letzten liebe

ich sagte schon so oft
china, wandern wir nach china aus
es ist dort spannend
spannender als hier
berlin war gestern
new york vorgestern
und sofia davor

dein ort — mein wort
der brauch

aus versehen
durch worte
wurde ich
deutscher als die deutschen
chinesischer als die chinesen

and giving birth to a german child is absolutely not enough
there's nothing german about being a woman
having a mother is not proof of citizenship
mothers only give birth
they beget nothing
they cannot bear witness

my word
your city

to turn your world into a word in me

how long is long enough for love?

let's start with 13
for superstition's sake

no bed and no money
just the country of my chance wanderings
of my last love

i've said so often
china, let's move to china
it's so exciting there
berlin was yesterday
new york the day before yesterday
and sofia the day before that

your world—my word
different things

accidentally
words
made me
more german than the germans
more chinese than the chinese

amerikanischer als die amerikaner
bulgarischer als die bulgaren
und so weiter
ich mag den unsinn ins groteske übertreiben

und vor allem –
wir sind lange genug hier gewesen
sogar wenn es nicht als lange genug gelten mag

es wird zeit

mein wort – dein ort

bevor es zu spät wird
bevor ich weniger deutsch werde
weniger bulgarisch, amerikanisch, chinesisch u.s.w.

wandern wir aus

jenseits

more american than the americans
more bulgarian than the bulgarians
and so on
i like to push nonsense into the grotesque

and anyway—
we've been here long enough
even if long enough isn't considered long enough

it's time

my word—your world

before it's too late
before i grow less german
less bulgarian, american, chinese etc.

let's move

beyond

VIADUKT

Über mich gehen viele Räder und Menschen
meine Arme und Beine sind gestreckt
mit Nägeln festgekrallt in den Sanddünen
meine Wirbel knacken nicht
wer hinübergeht kann ich nicht sehen
mein Gesicht starrt ins Wasser: Siddhartas Fluss

VIADUCT

Wheels and feet traverse me
my arms and legs are outstretched
nails dug into sand dunes
my vertebrae do not crack
I cannot see who is crossing
my face stares into the water: Siddhartha's river

DAS EINPFLANZEN DES GARTEN EDEN

„Nun, wie kann es gelingen, ein neues Paradies zu pflanzen?"
Johann Amos Comenius, 1592–1670

Die Leere ist Erinnerung an etwas,
was sein könnte oder der Wunsch ihrer Erfüllung.
Das Vorhandensein einer Abwesenheit,
bunt und breit.

Das Nichts ist düster, von der Größe her ungewiß,
eine Einladung, es zu bewohnen.

Die Null ist die Mitte der Waage,
der Minus- und Plus-Räume.
Ein Anfang, der immer da war,
und ein Ende, nur falls es akzeptiert wird.

Das Kind legt einen Kirschkern
zu jeder Rose, legt die ganze Kirsche
zu der Rosenbeere mit den Samen –
dann gießt es sie.

Wie schön ist dieser Kupferbehälter
zum Füllen,
und auch diese Luft, und diese Erde
in den Comenius-Gärten.

SOWING THE GARDEN OF EDEN

"How might we go about planting a new paradise?"
John Amos Comenius, 1592–1670

Emptiness is a reminder of something
that might exist, or the desire for its creation.
The presence of an absence,
colorful and capacious.

Nothingness is sinister, an unknown in terms of size;
it invites us to dwell in it.

Zero is the midpoint of the scale,
of the plus-minus spheres.
A beginning that was always there,
and an end, if one accepts it.

The child places a cherry stone
next to every rose, places the entire cherry
next to the roseberry with the seeds—
then it waters them.

This copper container that needs filling
is lovely,
and so is the air, and the earth
in the Comenius gardens.

Rustschuk, Russe, an der Donau

Zurück in die Zukunft
meiner früheren Vergangenheit.
Ich war neun als auf einer Kreuzung
in dieser Stadt der Verkehrspolizist freundlich
sagte: „Schneide deinen Weg gerade!"
als Antwort auf meine Frage, in welche Richtung
das Delta dieses Flusses zu erreichen wäre,
das damals so und so nicht zu erreichen war.
Am gegenüberliegenden Ufer die Fabrik,
eine andere unserer Vergangenheiten, eine
rumänische, der Stolz von Ceausescu,
das bedeutete keine Gegenwart, die
jene blaue, gelbe, graue, wunderbare
Luft über der Donau durchsichtiger macht —
Ökoglasnost fing dadurch an, meine Wende.

Ein Ausflug in die Zukunft
der vergangenen Zukunftsentwürfe.
Was erwartet mich dort bloß? Welche
Landrover und Mc's, welcher Donald am Steuer,
welche Zungen, die schon unsere Zungen —
meine und die von Canetti — gefressen haben,
im Tontopf gedünstet und stark gewürzt, um
ein Vergessen zu erleichtern. Das Vergessen,
dass sie heute erreichbar wären, das Delta
und auch die Quelle. Aber in Russe erscheinen
immer wieder Wegkundige und oft sind sie
wortreiche Engel, und ich achte auf ihre Worte,
schneide meinen Weg gerade,
und nähe mir einen Mantel aus Landkarten.
Er bringt mich zum Fliegen, und aus der Luft,
diesmal eine durchsichtigere, verwischen sich
Delta und Quelle, nur der Fluss ist zu sehen,

Ruschuk, Rousse, by the Danube

Back to the future
of my previous past.
I was nine when, at a junction
in this city, a friendly traffic policeman
said: "Cut your path straight!"
when I asked him how to
reach the delta of the river, which back then
could be reached neither one way nor the other.
On the opposite bank: the factory,
another of our pasts, a
Romanian one, the pride of Ceausescu,
it meant no present in which
that blue, yellow, grey, wonderful
air over the Danube is more transparent—
that's how Ekoglassnost began, my '89.

An excursion to the future
of bygone future plans.
What awaits me there? Which
Landrovers and Mc's, which Donald at the wheel,
which tongues that have already devoured
our tongues—mine and Canetti's—
braised in a pot of clay and heavily seasoned to
facilitate a forgetting. Forgetting
that you could reach them today, the delta
and the source. But in Rousse people
who know the way are always turning up, and they are often
verbose angels, and I heed their words,
cut my path straight,
and sew myself a coat of maps.
It allows me to fly, and from above—
this time the air is more transparent—delta and source
coalesce, there is only the river,

keine Vergangenheit, keine Zeit,
aus der Perspektive von Gertrud Stein
herrscht Klarheit über das Wasser,
das weder trennt, noch verbindet, nur fließt. Und ich
lande verwünscht am Meer, das mir den Papier-Mantel
auszieht und mich liebt. So einfach kann es sein,
wenn man nicht darauf besteht, dass es anders ist.

no past, no time.
From Gertrude Stein's perspective
clarity reigns over the water,
which neither separates, nor connects, only flows. And I
land, bewitched, by the sea, which takes off my paper coat
and loves me. That's how simple things can be
if you don't insist on their being otherwise.

Bewusst

Sie hat kein Haus, schwimmt überall im Ozean,
hat zwanzigtausend, die ihr genügen,
sie kennt den Schmerz und ihre eigenen Grenzen,
ist frei zu bewohnen und zu durchwandern,
sie liest das Meer und gebiert es neu,
ihre Nervenzellen reichen ihr zu erkennen.
Aplysia ist ein bewusstes Wesen.

Conscious

She has no house, swims all across the ocean,
has twenty thousand that will do,
she knows pain and her own borders,
is free to dwell and wander,
she reads the sea and gives birth to it again,
her nerve cells suffice for her to recognize.
Aplysia is a conscious being.

DER ANFANG UND DAS ENDE DER METAPHER

Hüh, Seepferdchen!
Atme
Vertrauen in den Tag.

THE BEGINNING AND THE END OF THE METAPHOR

Giddy up, sea horse!
Breathe
confidence into the day.

NOTES

Tzveta Sofronieva, who now predominantly writes poetry in German, also writes in Bulgarian and has occasionally written in English. Some of her poems were created in different languages simultaneously, and she has translated a number of her own poems, sometimes in collaboration with native-speaker editors. The first and second editions of *Eine Hand voll Wasser* were subtitled "Deutsche Gedichte" [German Poems] to indicate that the poems contained therein had been created in German, even if alternative "versions" happened to exist in other languages. The subtitle has been omitted from this bilingual edition to reflect the complexity of identifying a "source" text and the fact that the collection of poems has been altered slightly from its original presentation.

Eine Hand voll Wasser / A hand full of water: The italicized German text is taken from Wilhelm Müller's (1794–1827) poem "Das Wandern ist des Müllers Lust," which was set to music by Franz Schubert in the song cycle *Die schöne Müllerin*. The italicized Bulgarian text is from the Bulgarian folk song *Тръгнала Румяна за вода студена* [Tragnala Rumiana za voda studena].

Ein unbekanntes Wort / An unknown word: The German text borrows from the German children's rhyme "Wer kommt in meine Arme" and from the German children's song *Kommt ein Vogel geflogen*, as well as from the Bulgarian folk songs *Я кажи ми облаче ле бяло* [Ja kazhi mi oblache li bjalo] and *Гугутка гука в усои* [Gugutka guka v usoi]. Some of the lines in the English translation are taken from James Royce Shannon's (1881–1946) song "Too Ra Loo Ra Loo Ral (That's an Irish Lullaby)." Its use was inspired by an alternate English version of the poem, by the poet, which was published in *11 9 Web Streaming Poetry* (Auropolis Supernova: Belgrade, 2010). "An unknown word" exists in Bulgarian, German and English versions created by the poet.

Hurikan in Messembria / Hurricane in Mesembria: This poem was originally written in Bulgarian and published in the collection *Раз-познавания* (Zhanet45: Plovdiv, 2006). The English translation published here is based on the poet's own translation of the poem into German, which was published in the journal *transkrit* (2/2010).

Acknowledgements

The translator would like to thank the following organizations: PEN American Center, who supported this translation in the form of an award from the 2009 translation fund; The Banff International Literary Translation Centre, who supported the translation in the form of a residency in 2009; Mount Allison University, who provided financial support for the aforementioned residency; and The Cliff Becker Endowment for the Literary Arts for their support of this publication. She would also like to thank the poet, who turned a solitary endeavor into a dynamic dialogue.

About the Poet

A physicist and historian of science by training, Tzveta Sofronieva is the author of nine collections of poetry. She also writes short stories, essays and texts for the theater. Born in Sofia, Bulgaria, she settled in Berlin in 1992 but remains a frequent traveler. Sofronieva's first collection of poetry *Chicago Blues* (1992, bilingual, Bulgarian and English) was written during her travels through the US and Canada in 1989 and 1990. Among her most recent publications are a collection of short prose texts entitled *Diese Stadt kann auch weiß sein* (2010) and the poetry art book *Touch Me* (2012, bilingual, English and German). Her work also encompasses literary installations, the latest of which are *Borrowed Pillows* (Lille, France, 2011) and *My Cyborg Identity* (Boston, USA, 2012), and she has edited several anthologies, including *Forbidden Words* (2005) and *11 9 Webstreaming Poetry* (2010). She has translated poetry by Chris Abani, Margaret Atwood, Michael Krüger and Yoko Tawada into Bulgarian, among others. Her own work has been translated into a number of languages, among them French, Finnish, Hungarian, Polish, Serbian, Spanish and Uzbek.

Tzveta Sofronieva attended a master class with Joseph Brodsky in 1992. In 1988 she was awarded a prize for poetry by the Bulgarian Academy of Sciences. She has been writer-in-residence at the Academy Schloss Solitude in Stuttgart (1996), at KulturKontakt in Vienna (2003), at the Villa Aurora in Pacific Palisades (2005), and at the Max Planck Institute for the History of Science in Berlin (2010). In Spring 2012, she was Max Kade Writer-in-Residence at MIT in Boston.

Eine Hand voll Wasser (2008) was Tzveta Sofronieva's first full-length collection of poetry in German. In 2009 Sofronieva was awarded the *Adelbert-von-Chamisso-Förderpreis*, a prize given to German writers whose cultural background is not Germanic.

For more information visit www.tzveta-sofronieva.de.

ABOUT THE TRANSLATOR

Chantal Wright is Assistant Professor of German and Translation at the University of Wisconsin–Milwaukee. She grew up in Manchester, England, and studied at Girton College, Cambridge, and the University of East Anglia, Norwich.

The Cliff Becker Book Prize in Translation

> *"Translation is the medium through which American readers*
> *gain greater access to the world. By providing us with as direct*
> *a connection as possible to the individual voice of the author,*
> *translation provides a window into the heart of a culture."*
> —Cliff Becker, May 16, 2005

Cliff Becker (1964–2005) was the National Endowment for the Arts Literature Director from 1999 to 2005. He began his career at the NEA in 1992 as a literature specialist, was named Acting Director in 1997, and in 1999 became the NEA's Director of Literature.

The publication of this book of translation marks the culmination of work he had done in support of his personal passion for ensuring the arts are accessible to a wide audience and not completely subject to vagaries of the marketplace. During his tenure at the NEA, he expanded support for individual translators and led the development of the NEA Literature Translation Initiative. His efforts did not stop at the workplace, however. He carried out his passion in the kitchen as well as the board room. Cliff could often be seen at home relaxing in his favorite, worn-out, blue T-shirt, which read, "Art Saves Me!" He truly lived by this credo. To ensure that others got the chance to have their lives impacted by uncensored art, Cliff had hoped to create a foundation to support the literary arts which would not be subject to political changes or fluctuations in patronage, but would be marked solely for the purpose of supporting artists, and in particular, the creation and distribution of art which might not otherwise be available. While he could not achieve this goal in his short life time, now, seven years after his untimely passing, his vision has become manifest.

In collaboration with White Pine Press and the Cliff Becker Endowment for the Literary Arts, the Creative Writing Program at the University of Missouri, together with his surviving wife and daughter, has launched an annual publication prize in translation in his memory. The Cliff Becker Book Prize in Translation will produce one volume of literary translation in English, annually, beginning in the fall of 2012. It is our hope that with on-going donations to help grow the Becker Endowment for the Literary Arts, important artists will continue to touch, and perhaps save, lives of those whom they reach through the window of translation.